TRACE THE NUMBERS

1 2 3

NUMBERS & COUNTING WORKBOOK

AF270807

FOR PRESCHOOL & KINDERGARTEN

JUNE & LUCY kids

Email us at FREEBIES@JUNELUCY.COM
to get a FREE printable download!

FOR A LITTLE INSPIRATION
follow along at:

○ @JUNEANDLUCY

▢ @JUNEANDLUCY

WWW. JUNELUCY.COM

Shop our other books at
www.junelucy.com

Wholesale distribution through Ingram Content Group
www.ingramcontent.com/publishers/distribution/wholesale

For questions and customer service, email us at
support@junelucy.com

practice makes perfect
FREE DOWNLOAD!

WWW.JUNELUCY.COM/TTN2

@ @JUNEANDLUCY
f @JUNEANDLUCY

JUNE & LUCY kids

ONE

one

one one one one

one one one one

one one one one

one one one one

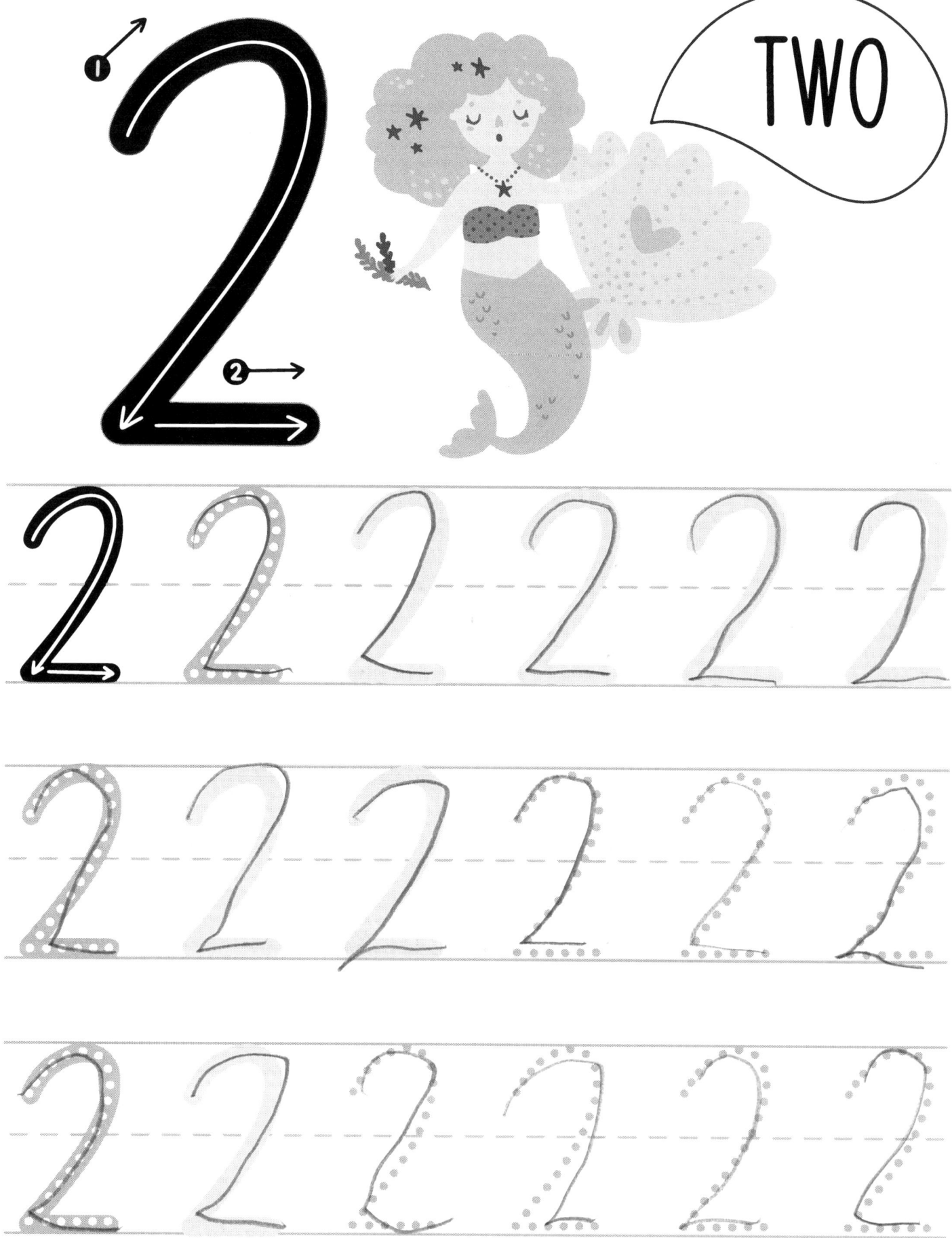

TWO

two

two two two

two two two

two two two

two two two

THREE

three

three

three

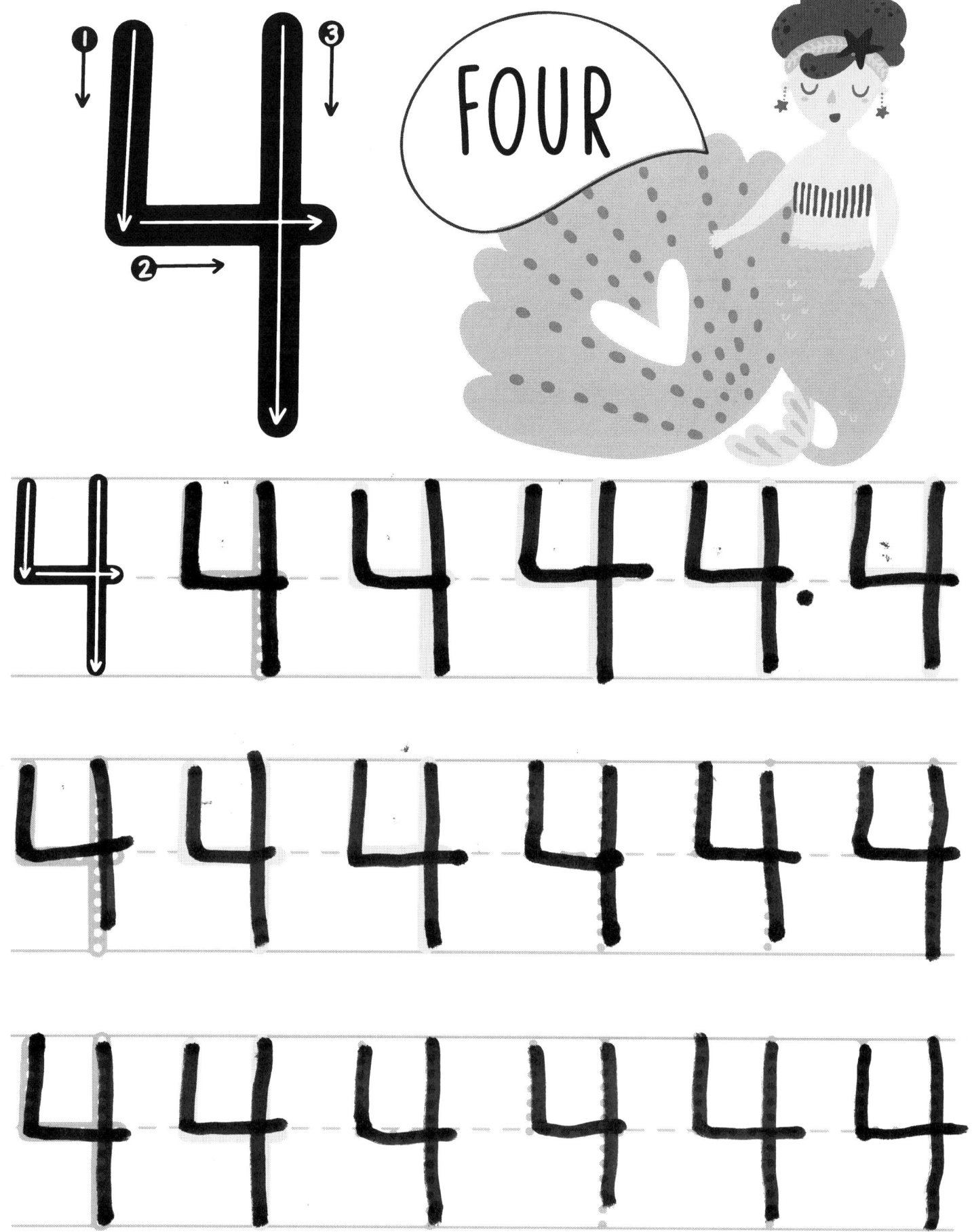

FOUR

four

four

four

four

four

FIVE

MAGICAL

five

five

five

five

five

6

SIX

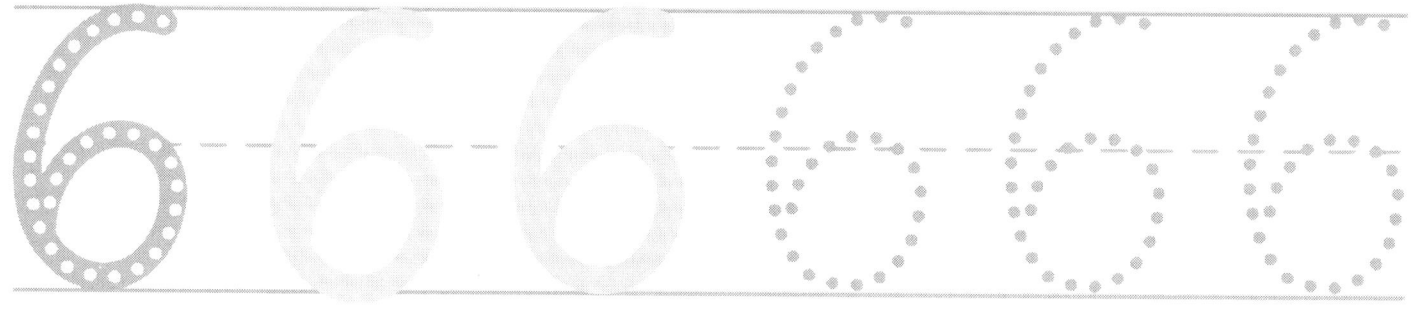

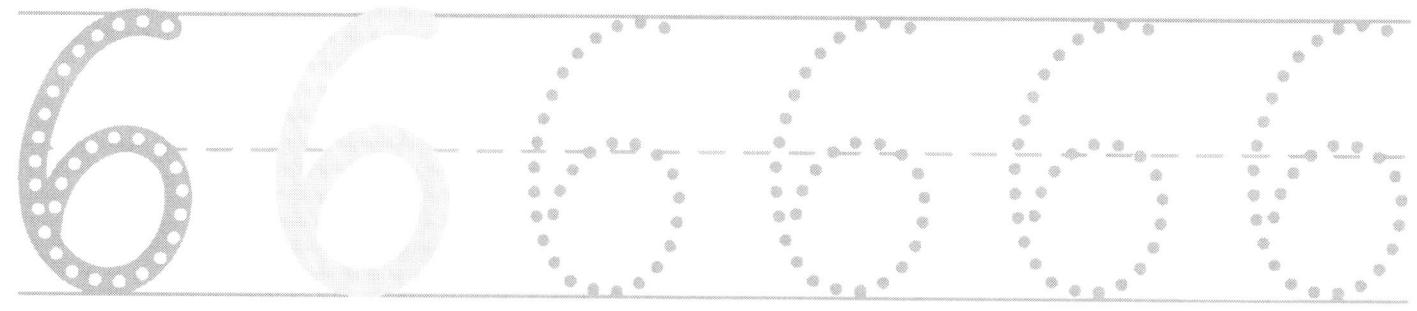

SEVEN

seven

seven

seven

seven

seven

EIGHT

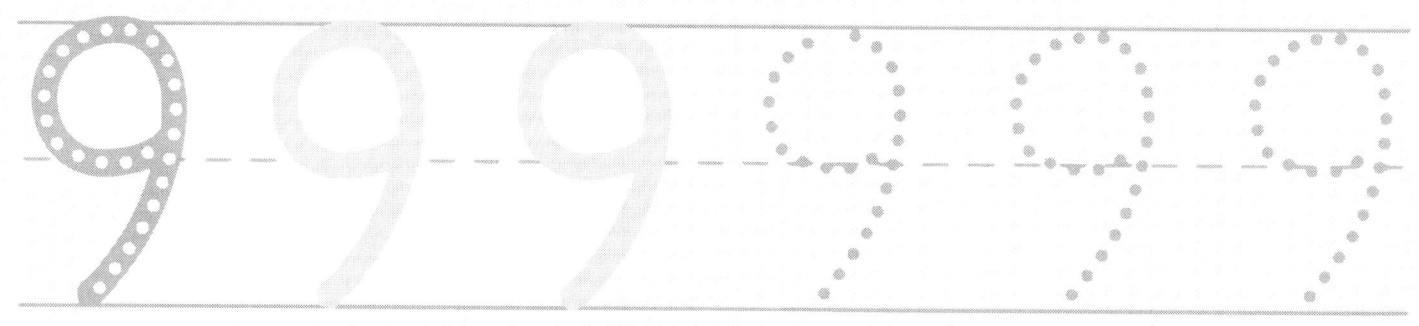

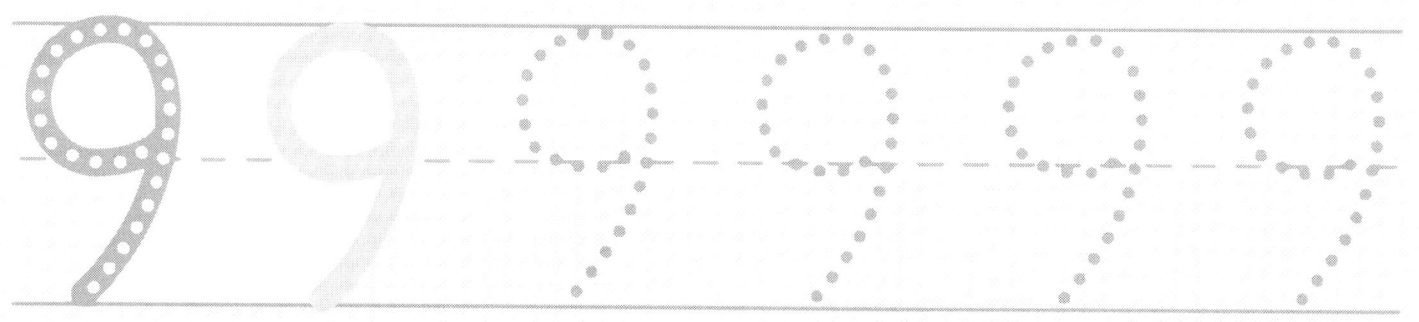

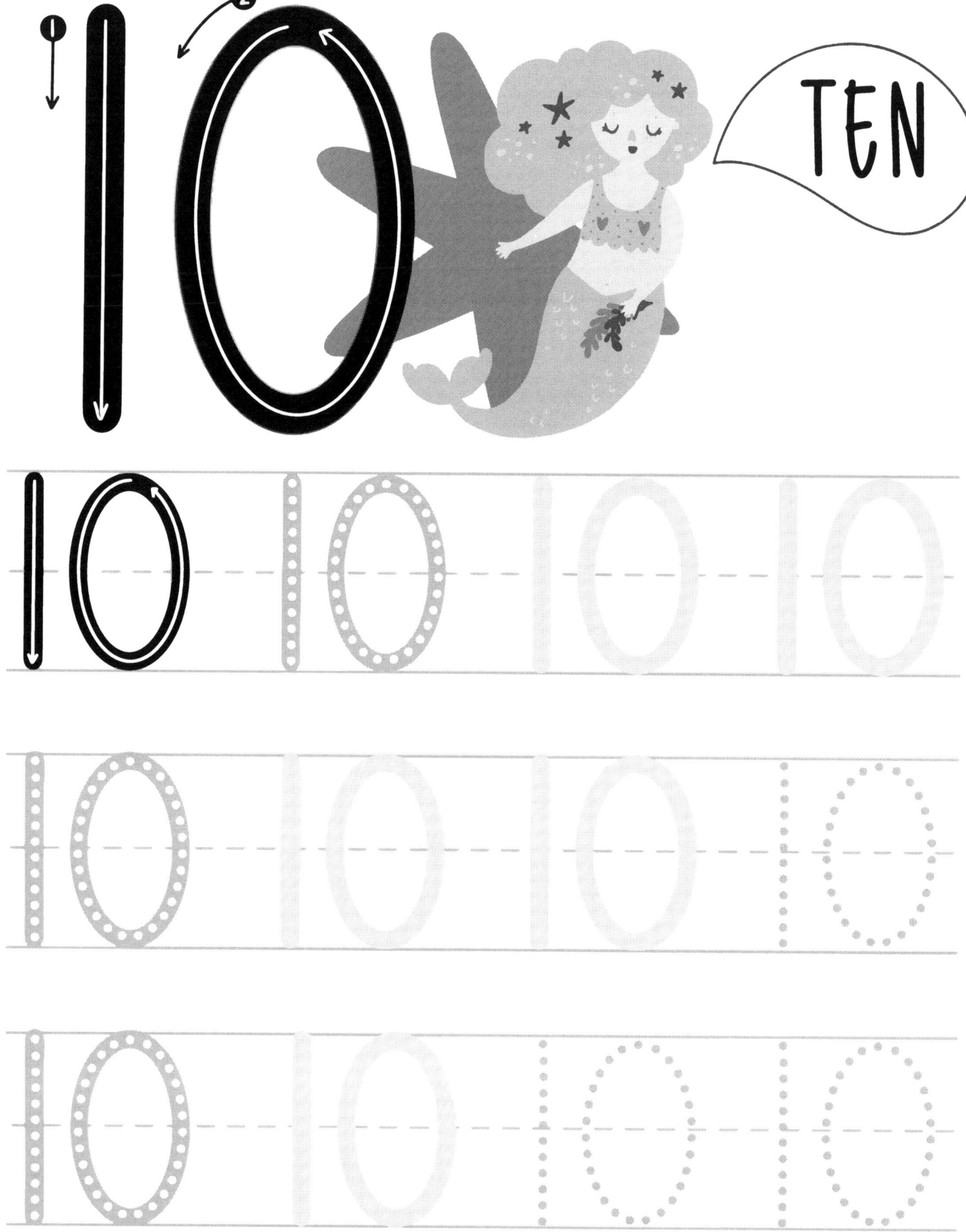

TEN

ELEVEN

eleven

TWELVE

THIRTEEN

FOURTEEN

fourteen

fourteen

fourteen

fourteen

fourteen

FIFTEEN

SIXTEEN

magical

sixteen

sixteen

sixteen

sixteen

sixteen

SEVENTEEN

believe in Magic

seventeen

seventeen

seventeen

seventeen

seventeen

EIGHTEEN

eighteen

eighteen

eighteen

eighteen

eighteen

NINETEEN

nineteen

20

TWENTY

Be a Mermaid and make waves

20 20 20 20

20 20 20 20

20 20 20 20

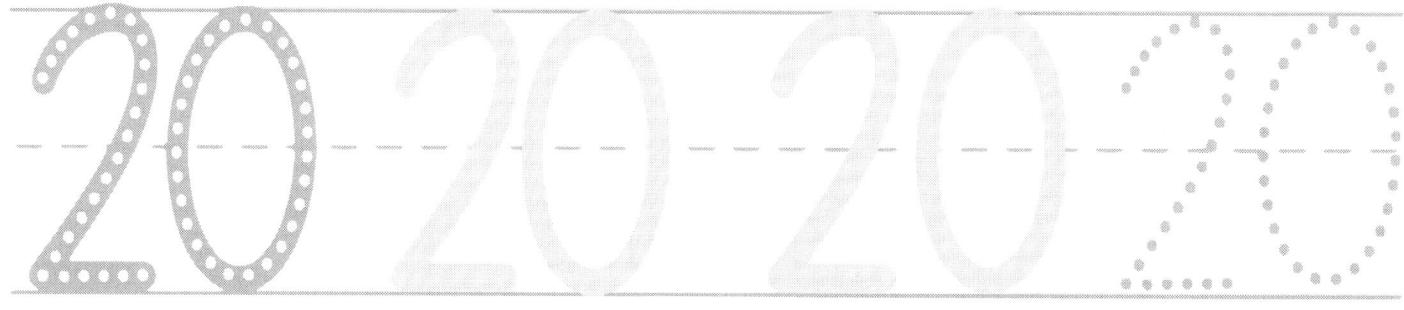

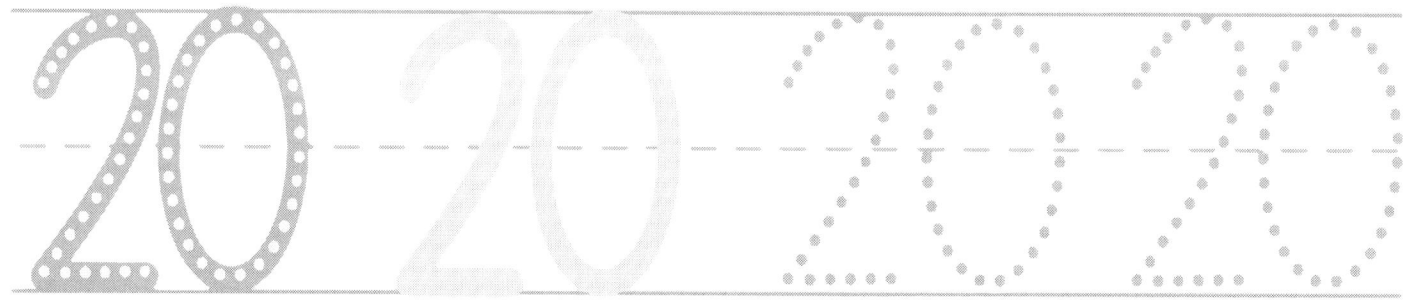

twenty

twenty

twenty

twenty

twenty

LET'S PRACTICE!
COUNTING

How many mermaids do you see?

_____ Mermaid!

mermaid

mermaid

How many bears do you see?

_____2_____ Bears!

2 bears

2 bears

How many cats do you see?

_____ Cats!

How many dinosaurs do you see?

_____ Dinosaurs!

4 dinosaurs

4 dinosaurs

How many elephants do you see?

_____ Elephants!

5 elephants

5 elephants

How many flamingos do you see?

_____ Flamingos!

6 flamingos

6 flamingos

How many giraffes do you see?

_____ Giraffes!

7 giraffes

7 giraffes

How many hippos do you see?

_____ Hippos!

8 hippos

8 hippos

How many iguanas do you see?

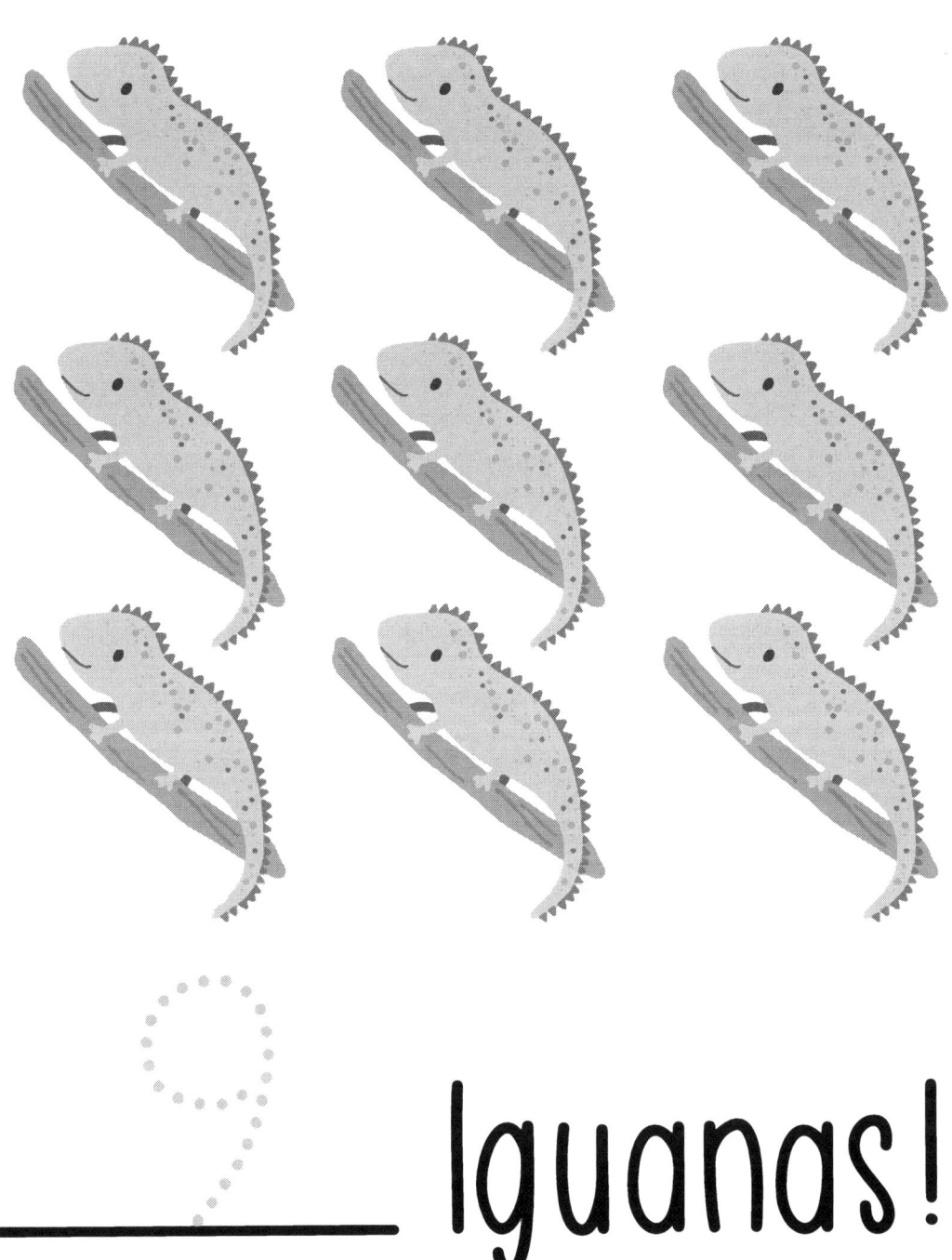

_____ Iguanas!

9 iguanas

9 iguanas

How many jellyfish do you see?

_____ Jellyfish!

10 jellyfish

10 jellyfish

How many koalas do you see?

_____ Koalas!

11 koalas

11 koalas

How many lions do you see?

_12_ Lions!

12 lions

12 lions

How many monkeys do you see?

_____ Monkeys!

13 monkeys

13 monkeys

How many narwhals do you see?

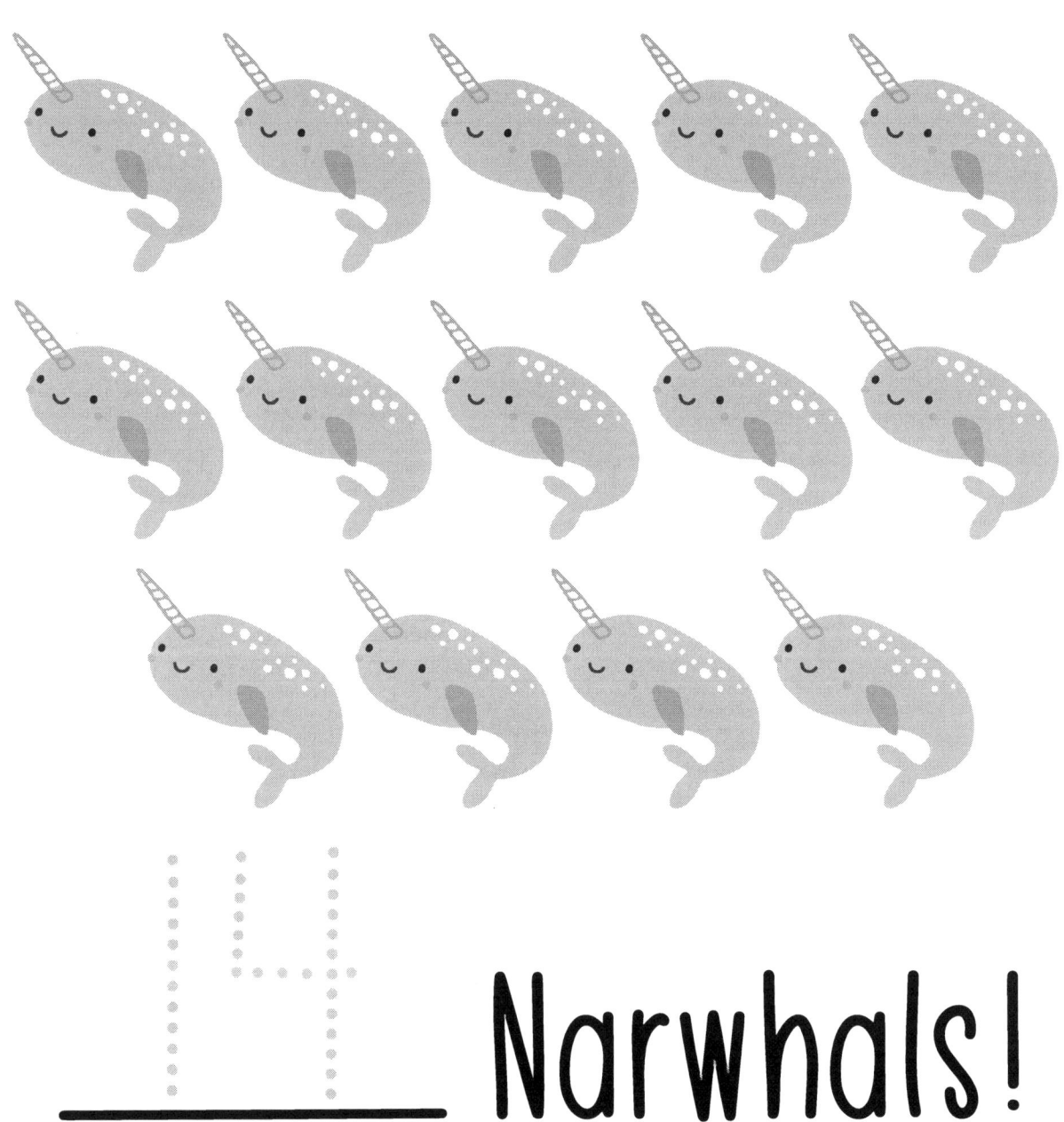

_____ Narwhals!

14 narwhals

14 narwhals

How many octopuses do you see?

_____ Octopuses!

15 octopuses

15 octopuses

How many penguins do you see?

_____16_____Penguins!

16 penguins

16 penguins

How many quail do you see?

_____ Quail!

17 quail

17 quail

How many raccoons do you see?

_____ Raccoons!

18 raccoons

18 raccoons

How many snails do you see?

_____ Snails!

19 snails

19 snails

How many turtles do you see?

_____ Turtles!

20 turtles

20 turtles

Made in the USA
San Bernardino, CA
10 August 2020